TOWN
LIFE

Other Books by Jay Parini

Singing in Time (poetry)
Theodore Roethke: An American Romantic (criticism)
The Love Run (novel)
Anthracite Country (poetry)
The Patch Boys (novel)
An Invitation to Poetry (textbook)

TOWN LIFE

POEMS

Jay Parini

AN OWL BOOK

HENRY HOLT AND COMPANY — NEW YORK

Published by Henry Holt and Company, Inc.,
521 Fifth Avenue, New York, New York 10175.
Published in Canada by Fitzhenry & Whiteside Limited,
195 Allstate Parkway, Markham, Ontario L3R 4T8.

Library of Congress Cataloging-in-Publication Data
Parini, Jay.
Town life.
"An Owl book."
I. Title.
PS3566.A65T69   1988   811'.54   87-11907
ISBN: 0-8050-0577-3 (pbk.)

First Edition

Designed by Jeffrey L. Ward
Printed in the United States of America
1   3   5   7   9   10   8   6   4   2

ISBN 0-8050-0577-3

For Devon, *sempre*

ACKNOWLEDGMENTS

"The Mariner" and "Town Life" first appeared in *Poetry*. "The Visitors" first appeared in *The Hudson Review*. Other poems first appeared in the following publications: *The American Scholar, Boston Review, The Bread Loaf Anthology of Contemporary Poetry, Chicago Review, Graham House Review, The Hudson Review, Michigan Quarterly Review, The Missouri Review, New England Review and Bread Loaf Quarterly, The New Republic, Ontario Review, Oxford Poetry, The Partisan Review, Seagate II, The Southern Review, Verse, Virginia Quarterly Review,* and *The Yale Review*.

CONTENTS

III. Portraits of the Artist

IV. Divine Parameters

TOWN
LIFE

The Mariner

for Richard Kenney

This wide-plank skiff of a table
is rigged for travel,
with a sunny window at my back.
I sit alone here, spinning
an old globe beside my chair, its skin
of colors, planet of my own.
I list the places I would go:
the outer regions of my hands,
the tiny nerve-ends twitching in the night,
the peninsular foot, the nether bowels,
the mucous caverns of my inner ear.
I set my sails each morning after breakfast,
pulling sheets from a left-hand drawer,
taking a pen between my teeth.
The spirits seem to blow
four ways at once or, mostly, not at all.
Even Agamemnon had to slay a daughter
just for winds to carry him to Troy.
I, too, have slaughtered my kin
for motion, for a poem to waste.
Now I spread my charts,
correct my compass, and lay down a course
through the next few hours.
May the gods who brood upon these waters
ease my way, direct the passage
of this fragile craft,
this sloop of self I angle into day.

I

I

In the Sphere of Common Duty

Most blameless is he, centered in the sphere
Of common duties, decent not to fail
In offices of tenderness, and pay
Meet adoration to my household gods,
When I am gone.

—Tennyson, "Ulysses"

Syrinx

A summer glebe
at zero noon.
Syrinx—the sound
of pipes across
a weedy pond
unrustles trees.
I wonder if
the sound I think
I heard was real
or not, as in
that wet glade
where Pan discerned
a wilder note
and waded into
water thick
with reeds. That day
he lay as if
unmade against
a mossbank, trying
to recall a note
more overheard
than heard, a sleight
of wind, a sudden
rightness passing.

The Conception

Wind slips, catlike,
through the trees.
Cold snap at dawn.
One podlike sparrow
clings to brush:
a pericarp in winter.
Sheets we've slept in
through a night of love
now cool with absence
of our lengthened forms,
that night of starburst,
whorl, the lifted
cotta-like white cotton
gown. Was one
seed sown? Outside,
we track the brittle grass;
we suck sharp air.
The house behind us
dwindles in a huff
of breath, blown snow.

Off into woods:
our snowshoe thuds
compete with nothing
but the winter heart's
white, muffled tick.
We climb all morning.
Well above the town,
we look into a field
furled in the surplice
of a full month's snow:

cold rock once fire,
a feldspar cauldron,
igneous and running.
What are we, you say,
but lava, leaving
traces that will cool
for those, the wished-for
children of your womb?

I pluck a pod,
a furball ovum,
from a bone-white
bush; I rub it
till the red seeds
stain my fingers.
Soft words hang like
smoke-wreaths in the air.

You take my hand
(the gloveless hand)
inside your sweater,
hot and moist. Your belly
seems alive in my wet palm:
in leafless weather,
in the blank of winter,
as the moth-wing snow
flakes off high branches,
and the unseen roots
begin to swirl.

The Visitors

Our children sleep among the stars:
blunt, bodiless, unnamed.
The music of their sphere is one long vowel.
None has been signaled from the ground by us,
at least not yet.
Mere argument will never bring them down,
since accidental entry is their mode,
a rupture into flesh,
the starlight overhead past recollection.
Their going will be difficult as well:
a disremembering, consonants disowned.
That change will hurt like every other change.
Only in the spring,
when new grass skims a sudden world,
will any of them understand our need,
our wishing we could hold them,
say their names and set them down.

Differentiation

Already the brow begins to knit,
the arm-buds reach for freedom from the mass,
the eyeholes deepen.

Delicate, the spine uncurls and lengthens,
ganglia and nerves by slow degrees
inhabit what we used to call the soul.

A small pulse separates on its own time,
and none of this is me,
or you, or us.

Brainwaves scatter in the blank of night,
a splay of light from
some new star.

And gently in the amniotic drowse
its face begins to shine,
a lucent stare.

Soon every feature will believe its name,
and tight fists beat across
the broken water.

Crops

And there is sadness in the way they grow—
bell peppers at full gong in mid-July,
the corn breast-high
where mudprints followed me uphill in May,
loud snapping fingers, peas or beans,
the feathery and light-engorging dill,
the long-haired chives or rough-tongued mint,
engaging basil,
my fair son,
his tendril body climbing through the air.

History

History has many corridors, yes,
and floodlit stages where the folks
with greater parts than we have
romp, cavort, and trade bold gestures
that affect us all,
and sooty alleys where you'd only go
for love or money;
it's a steeply winding stair,
a sliding board, a tunnel or a ramp,
depending on your gravity of mind
or point of view—but all
the same, the level years
like floors that tumble through a burning house
and come to rest, blue cinders,
on the ground where all things subject
to the laws of change must come to rest,
the shelf of now,
this moment over breakfast
as we touch warm fingers over
toast and jam
and say, okay, I'm glad you're here,
no matter what we said or did before,
I'm glad you're here.

Another Version of Our Love

in Minnesota

We crossed the water over midnight
waves, the two of us,

revising once again,
with Norway pines like pencils

on the moon-white parchment,
scribbling for our lives.

I hauled our boat up
on the bank beside a willow

with its braids undone.
We found each other, slowly,

in the cabin dark;
we reached like willow roots

for water, more sweet water,
trying to recall

some version of our love
lost in those woods

a time before.
The log fire slumped

from wood to ash,
as night's swift shuttle

.

pierced the loom,
and we woke blackened in our limbs

at dawn, the fire-pit drawn,
all passion spent

in crumpled sheets we'd cast away,
the rain like smolder

on the pine-tarred roof,
the cabin drafty, cold and bare.

Lullaby

Hang on, my dear, in glooms of day,
through sopping noons, this season
of pure wistfulness, regret,
the pooling grays, till reason
comforts in its northern way
with kind inductions that foretell
relief, insisting that what's wet
must one day dry, that summers past
augur that nothing cold can last
forever, even frozen hell.

Panglossian? Perhaps. Lock fingers
with me now, as dark surrounds
the house, as slantwise rain
licks at the roof, and a wilder sound—
the dog-torn wind—malingers.
Weather is a feint, trumped up
by spirits who delight in dishing pain,
who seem to need to test our love,
as if, mere mortals, we must prove
resistant to climatic flux.

Fidelity, like certainty,
exists, but only in the mind of God;
let each of us profess, oh, just
enough for comfort as we trod
those ways to death: eternity
may last a longish time. Let's risk
whatever we both think we must
to keep us lively in the gloomy hours,

the tedium that often overpowers,
this winter weather, wet and brisk.

All weather, in the end, will look
unreal to lovers in repose who, reading
backward, skim the years for lapses
of affection, sleights of heart, confessing
to each other how each took
advantage and, when put upon,
complained. Forgive our lapses,
mine and yours. Let passions override
this drizzle that we can't abide.
In glooms of day, my dear, hang on.

The Hippocamp

for Gore Vidal

The hippocamp is yours, its primal image
on the wall, cut out of time, the antique tile
a kind of host to something it cannot
quite understand, this endlessly defiant,
deaf, dark seahorse hanging fire,
a miniature dragon, head erect
against all comers: waves, ill winds,
whatever in the surf intends to fault
a lofty balance that, perforce, endures.

Perforce because its legend, like your own,
admits no upset—tailspin, sprawl. You rise
or fall within the wave's translucent aura,
which becomes your shimmering façade,
brocade of self. Breast high and tilting
skyward on a large, white-crested wave,
you baffle us with changes: minotaur
or centaur, hippogriff or wyvern, shifting
as the surf around you shatters, shelves.

Who understands, at last, why species fail,
why some are pitched and tossed like minnows
in a rasping spray, yet some must shark
the depths forever, foil and feed, while others
seem to hover, fed on, foiled, unable
to adapt to local color or defend their nests?
Who gave the squid its power to obscure
the world and, so, withdraw, or you such balance
that the crumbling waters ease your fall?

The Way Out

With moonlight on the tracks
beside the river, standing
in my grandma's garden after dusk,
the uncut grass is blue
about my knees. It's late
September, and the vines
of overripe tomatoes
sag and bleed, brown lettuces
and kale already mulching
in the grainy dirt as fireflies
pop in lungs of willows,
and a mottled pear crop
scents the air. The river
has a mouth to tell its tale,
but who'll tell hers?
As black wings flutter
and the long dark roosts,
I strain to see her
as she walks the tracks beyond
her garden into open fields,
with rails converging
where the heart stops cold.

Goodnight, Goodnight

Goodnight, sweet women I have loved

   too little or too late

Bright hair, bright fingernail and bone

              Goodnight, goodnight

On shores of darkness, one by one
the house-lights flicker
as you lay your heads on ice or cloud

   Too near or far

              Goodnight, goodnight

I think of you asleep in far-off cities
with your downy covers drawn up close
a gathering of smells and tastes I've lost

goodnight, sweet losses

   As the wolves bay shadows on the distant steppes
   as bears eat snow
   as black hawks circle for a place to land
   how far away you seem

your tendrilous pale fingers
kisses, kindnesses
the ill-timed jokes or passing jibes

Forgive me   I forgive

  our tastelessness and ignorance and fear
  our reckless humor, raucous cries

Let each of us, when night falls once for last
rise up and float together, me and you
sucked easily as fly-ash up the flue

In the Sphere of Common Duty

Telemachus did well, I think, to stay,
in spite of what his father might have said
about the promise written in the stars.
The island was all right, nothing fantastic,
but he called it home, then made it home
by taking on himself the fond discharge
of homely duties—taking out the trash,
deciding which of nature's green-leaved things
one should call "weeds" and separate to mulch,
accepting that it's infinitely harder
to stay put than rush away. Ulysses would have
loved the grand illusion that adventures hang
on precipices, passions, clashing rocks:
the crude near-misses of the manly life;
he went off to war, as men still do,
for reasons the community allowed
were just and not just his. But once the Trojans
had been done to death: What then? What then?
"Boys will be boys," they always say.
Think of him, Telemachus, who loved the stars
no less for watching them from where he stood.

Reading Through the Night

Late reading, and our books dissolve
in thunder, lightning through the rain;
their lights burn single in the mind.

Your novel and my novel move together,
line by line, like Noah's animals,
who found the ark, each other as the flood-

tide rose. Our oaky bed, its headboard
of a prow, lifts over waves. Your hero
and my heroine engage, as night whelms over

and the one great plot, that salty stew,
as ever, thickens. In a single sheet, we feel
the rise and fall of breath, the generations

that have come and gone and come again.
Is nothing ever lost? Eternal climax,
denouement: we find ourselves, at dawn,

on that bare hillside, disembarked,
the animals afoot, our novels turning
on themselves again, their separate spines.

Skiing Home at Dusk

This is the blessed hour when shadows lengthen
on the blue-red snow, when skiers mount
the billows with an ease, a forward *shush,*

and memory excites the tilt toward home:
the woody fire that blossoms over logs,
the candle and the book, hibernal harvest.

Motion through the trees collects the soul,
a whispering in transit, wind that's caught
like music in a flute's brief wooden throat.

This is the hour of accepted grace,
when everywhere we've been comes down to this:
the edge of day, where particles of thought

cohere like atoms in a structured dance
around one center that we call ourselves,
like poetry: the patterned perfect dance

of sentences that rise and fall with sense,
a language adequate to what we see
and feel and hear, a broad equivalence,

the center of the mind as clear as winter
with its empty backlit bedrock sky,
the motes of snow-dust blowing in the trees.

This is the hour when skiers and their skis
make one crisp sound, when every object
revels in its name, when *home* is home.

II

Town Life

Town Life

for Ann Beattie

It strikes me as the best of every world
this morning as I leave the house at nine
and walk uptown, past shuttered houses
I have learned by heart down to the angle
of each sloping roof, the kinds of siding
and their various degrees of disrepair.
I've memorized the shrubbery and lawns,
all so reflective of their owners' minds,
the blend of trees, some planted by the town
in 1920, others here by chance,
the drift of wind, or someone's purpose.
Today September-blooming mountain laurels
burn with flowers to fill the gaps where long-
necked elms once made a tunnel of their leaves.
I know this sidewalk as a blind man knows
his way around his rooms: the tilting flagstones
and the gravel drives, macadam stretches
that will heave with frost by mid-December.
All my joints adjust to ups and downs
as I proceed, half drunk on air, on night-
rinsed grasses and the gilt-edged leaves
that riffle in the slightest wind with that
low rustling tinny note of early fall,
the note of loss that makes me savor
what befalls each step: the wedge of geese
that arrows overhead between slate roofs,
the exoskeletons of huge black ants
that file like soldiers through the Khyber Pass
to certain failure in the winter's grip,
the squirrels rippling in gray blurs up trees
with preservations in their iron jaws.

There's so much going on I'll never know
but happily assume has its own pattern;
I have mine, which fits into the town's
slow ritual so well no doubt you'll wonder
if some parts of me were not lopped off
to make this fitting. Wouldn't I prefer
to wake at dawn in country heaven, with acres
of raw land around my house, with crops to tend,
with cows dewlapping through the shallow swales?
Some friends saw wood to save their souls
while I burn oil; they hike into the hills
for rustic solace as I walk these streets.
I've other friends who live in cities and believe
in motion multiplied by time, the swirl
of faces, calendars with no blank spaces left.
Their lives are vertical, like glass and steel,
and full of light at any time of day.
I don't begrudge them what they've found to work.
I'm all for anything that makes you feel
the gravity afoot, the tug of light
particulars, the sway of chosen hours,
though I love town life for its lazy Susan
of well-timed events, the tower that chimes,
the surge of traffic at appointed moments,
life in slow concentric circles that acknowledge
morning, noon, and night, imperious seasons
that enforce their rules, make us accede
to larger motions than we make ourselves.
I love the neighborliness of little towns,
the expectations that are so well met:
the waitress at the diner where I drink

my de-caf coffee, one old cop who never
says hello, too charged with duty to descend
to pleasantries on county time, the dozen
keepers of the dozen shops who fill my life
with necessary objects, foods, and service.
Their worlds depend upon my morning walk,
my needs and whims. And so we live in
symbiotic swirl around the center
of the village green: its white gazebo
like a hub of sorts, the centrifugal
aim of all our motion, though it's really
useless as a building goes, except for
concerts by the local bands on summer nights.
That white gazebo is the town's real heart:
a minor symbol of nostalgic longing
for our fictive past amid the hubbub
of our daily work in buildings shaped
to useful ends: the Greco-Roman banks
with much more cash than any of us needs
to make one life, the small post office
that can ship our mail to Bognor Regis
or Addis Ababa without any hitch.
It seems that we can eat our cake and have it,
though all wisdom votes against that fact.
I use the royal "we" perhaps too glibly,
since I'll never stand for public office
or consent to join the Rotary or Masons.
(My love of town life doesn't go that far.)
Whatever else I do, I'll fill these streets
with all the shambling presence I can muster
for enough good years to say I've been here

and have met them well on equal terms.
I'll be one spoke in this bright wheel
that spins through decades at its chosen speed,
that passing airplanes notice like a dime
in heavy grass—a glint of silver—
something they would probably pick up
if only it were not so far away.

Suburban Swamp

The swamp at the end of our cozy county road
does nothing for the value of what we own;
it's what the agents call an eyesore
and the neighbors never mention to their friends,
half wishing what they never set in words
will not exist. I'm standing by the stumps
that fizzle like antacid tabs in water,
the tatty oaks too old for leaves, loose
at the roots like blackened teeth that wobble
in the gums, a periodontal nightmare.
This was once a lake, old-timers say,
remembering the sunny Sunday picnics
where these mossbanks grow or, some say,
"fester." Frogs exhale into the midday air.
The green-gold water pops its blisters.
Winds are redolent of larval scum
that might well be a soothing balm for backache
in an old wives' tale if old wives lived.
The Indians came out in bark canoes
two centuries ago; now Boy Scouts tramp
the margins for a merit badge or two,
birdwatchers wait for oddly feathered friends,
and secret moralists inspect the setting
for its sheer decay. I like it how
what happens happens out of sight here.
Business goes on beneath the surface:
transformations: water into froth,
great hulking logs to pulp and steam.
Here every change is hidden but complete,
all purposes obscured—a skilled dismantling,
de-creation into light and air.

The Function of Winter

I'm for it, as the last leaves shred
or powder on the floor, as sparrows find
the driest footing, and November rains
fall hard as salt sprayed over roads.
The circulating spores take cover
where they can, and light runs level
to the ground again: no more the vertical
blond summer sheen that occupies a day,
but winter flatness—light as part of things,
not things themselves. My heart's in storage
for the six-month siege we're in for here,
laid up for use a little at a time
like hardtack on a polar expedition,
coveted though stale. Ideas, which in
summer hung a crazy jungle in my head,
subside now, separate and gleam in parts;
I braid them for display on winter walls
like garlic tails or onions, crisp bay wreaths.
One by one, I'll pluck them into spring.
If truth be told, I find it easier
to live this way: the fructifying boom
of summer over, wild birds gone, and wind
along the ground where cuffs can feel it.
Everything's in reach or neatly labeled
on my basement shelves. I'm ready to begin
to see what happened when my heart was hot,
my head too dazzled by itself to think.

A Lost Topography

Starfall, backfill—
home again: the headlamps flicker on the dumps,
the backhoes leveling
the once-bright culm that filled the air
with reek of memory, the red-
blue hills of April dusk,
when I would walk this way from school,
imagining the lives ploughed under, lost,
the phosphorescent names
like Nanticoke or Pittston, Moosic or Old Forge.
If only I could count the stars that fell here,
fell and cooled,
resumed a lusterless composure
on this sandy field, a rich moraine
where moonwort thrives, where thistle and white mold
become an overlay, where substance
crumbles and the pigeons gloom.

Passing Through Vermont on Three Martinis

For purple miles the mountains rise
above the river. Barns
assemble in surrounding corn.
The traveler takes nothing here for granted,
tippling under ice-and-vodka skies.
He listens to the water's racy babble
and discerns a meaning. Even
when the wind yanks back a shutter,
he perceives a sign. A farm boy
fishing in the distance moves him
more than a museum. Cowbells
tinkle in the distant calm.
He vows to quit his salaried position
one fine day, returning to this spot
to sip forever as the mountains rise.

Piazza

Life circulates here, watched
only by the random few:
the tourist with her blank regard
or a conqueror passing through.

It's a square, sometimes a circle
or a wobbly tetrahedron,
channeling the cars, the kindly
chatter going on and on.

All know one truth, that nothing
appertains beyond
this circus, and the human
commerce it depends on.

All love the hubbub, which connotes
success in multiples
of children, Vespas, coins,
the slick materials

the young must wear to track
the eyes of other young,
young men and women
who will loll their tongue

and live on wheels, a Honda
or a Fiat, maybe just
a bike; the point's in wheeling it—
it's move or bust.

Life seems so easy if one lets
the fountain's water-spouting

breasts become a focus,
if one lets the shouting

fill the ears with operatic
tones of bull or barter,
the pervasive tease, the snub,
the genially senseless banter

of the balding lad who cuts
a brutish figure in the crowd
but nonetheless is loved
by Mamma, who's serenely proud

he keeps a wife and wears
silk shirts. Who cares,
they seem to say, if politics
are local, or if pairs

of lovers are the only sight
worth dreaming when, at last,
one goes to bed? Tomorrow,
what-has-been becomes the Past

and therefore boring. Life
is what comes next, and how
one meets it, preferably poised,
applauding every bow.

America

How could I forget you, with your peaks
like compound fractures poking through the skin,
your svelte, deciduously fluttering trees
and conifers that bristle, jacked with light
on chilly slopes: blue western mountains
I have flown above but never hiked?
How could I ignore your gainly rivers—
Merrimack and Hudson, Mississippi,
with their slender reefs and ox-bow turns,
Ohio, Delaware, and Susquehanna—
on and on, running with grandiloquent
profusion through the grassy lands? They seem
restrained, for all their grandeur, almost as if
they understood their place in commerce even more
than nature and would not obstruct the flow
of goods, unlike unruly counterparts elsewhere:
the Ganges or the Nile, who regularly
drown whole populations, or the useless Congo,
pouring through a smoke of stinging flies,
or the Thames and Seine, content to lie
forever in repose reflecting spires,
flying buttresses, and gargoyle faces
that inspire a nation to adore its past
more than its future, unlike you,
who never gave a whit for history except
as something you could sell to eager tours
in Williamsburg or Boston—legendary homes
with brassy plaques and monumental stares.
You were always one to yearn toward,
excited by the thought of pure production,
the freedom to expand, revise old parts,

create a mall where mills once rattled
through their ten-hour shifts, transform
a dingy tenement to flats and quaint
boutiques, unfazed by barriers of brick
or finance. You advance by instinct, gifted
with a swift, revisionary mind that won't
let go. I know you by your restlessness
and brooding: smokestacks smudging up the sky,
the ten-lane highways that converge and tangle
in spaghetti loops, the open roads
that make a desert one more backdrop
as the trucks roll by, the buses, cars.
You're driven by a glad and giddy heart
that's open to the world and wants the world
to imitate your broad, successful gestures
and be rich as you are, clean and free.
All poverty and weakness hide their eyes
in your hard glare, are driven into corners,
left to mourn or fester out of sight.
I'd know you anywhere, my dashing country,
who can never say *enough,* who watches me
like Mom, believing that my fate is yours
as well. You let me breathe you and become
your body, linger in your arms, or leave you
for another, far-off country, where
the customs differ and your name is mud.
But then you welcome me, a rebel son
come home again to join the work at hand,
this fond production that becomes a story
you will never read but cherish nonetheless.

The White Town

I often think of Hannibal,
the white town of my childhood.   —*Mark Twain*

It glitters like a piece of glass in dirt
as light careens off steeples, slated roofs,
the balconies with newly painted rails.
The silent children scatter through the leaves,
and sidewalks bristle with the whitest ants,
pale cats and dogs, the dovelike pigeons;
chalk-dust streets give way to gravel
as the milk trucks sway beyond town lines.
The mothers in their homes stay out of sight,
the fathers working in another state.
Unfazed by change or coloring or death,
the white town spins through unmarked time.
I feel its shimmer in the midlife mind
like winter sunlight through a double-glaze,
a towny heartland underneath the haze,
its whirling pigments in a pinwheel dream
mixed white in memory: an ashy blend
of beet-red leaves and blue-black cinders,
blue-vermilion culm and azure slag,
the mud-brown cellarholes and mucous glades
with lilies overlaid, the orangeade suns—
all ground to powder, into soft dry snow,
the frosted window you can never open.

III

Portraits of the Artist

Portrait of the Artist at Baptism

in Scranton, 1960

The window rose, its blood-bright colors back-lit
  by the Sunday-morning sun,
    the hands of Christ
nail-wounded, reaching, open-palmed
above my twelve-year-old reflection

in the tepid pool behind the pulpit;
  angel-gowned, my underwear
    restraining manhood's
  bold defiant bulge, I stood
in front of hundreds who would watch me sink

past sin, past groin-thoughts, past old ways,
  drown one body to begin
    anew, a new
  man, rise as Jesus did
Himself in that dove-wimpled, curling stream.

The calla lilies trumpeted my rise,
  that resurrection to a life
    of infinite
  regression, to the long backslide
from now to then, my certain putrefaction.

I've been through it since, gone deep in waters
  of my own contrivance, fallen
    over falls, on jag-
  toothed rocks of selfishness and greed,
refusals to acknowledge what was other

and, therefore, divine. I have been reborn
  a thousand times, in daily

rituals of douse
and drown, unwittingly reborn,
if not forgiven, as on that wild day

amid the riffling of a hundred whispers,
organ blast and blood-
shine's splatter
on my face and hands—when I rose
toward light, the dripping promise of a life to come.

Portrait of the Artist on the Mound

in Scranton, 1963

That was my last game, me on the mound
  in white, green-capped,
    a lefty, hurling
  in the red-smoke dusk for extra innings,
as the game went on and on and on.

Was it really me? I felt dislodged there,
  looking down on that dull
    center of
  a whirling diamond: Father in
the stands, a white moon rising like a fastball, high.

One by one they faced me as I sought
  the zone, the abstract point
    of no return,
  releasing into air my leathery
and knuckle-rasping pitch, my contact with the world

outside the whorl I carried with me, the confusing
  schemes of power and glory,
    halls of fame,
  the manageable yet so unfounded
fear that maybe I would win and not deserve it.

With this team behind me, who could lose?
  I thought, while losing,
    as the ball struck
  bone-wood, crack, loose splinters
and the blur of dust, runs batted in.

Was I really weeping? No one saw,
  the culm dumps burning in a ring

around the field
like pink, sore flesh around a wound.
The coach, like God, just wouldn't take me out.

The backstop held me in its cross-hatched net,
   the sun, along a narrow
     squint-line, thumbed
   my eyes, the miners' children cheering
in the dusky rose-bowl stadium of night.

Portrait of the Artist as Revolutionary

in Washington, D.C., 1967

Bandana on my brow, tight jeans
  below a tie-dyed shirt,
    I detested war
  and Lyndon Johnson, "Scourge of Asia,"
and the world aflame inside my head.

Just one of them, the hippies on parade:
  we shouted, "Hell, no,
    we won't go!"
  to Vietnam, wherever. Young
and foolish, we were right, of course.

By accident, perhaps. Unfit for service by,
  if not real conscience,
    realer fear,
  we were much too smart to follow,
and assumed small risks and marched toward

the Future unaware that time would thin
  our ranks, as some of us
    made love, and others,
  money, as the granite buildings
filled with Us, not only Them, the over-

thirty. Sad, looking back, how we shrink
  and cringe, imagining
    the Past requires
  excuses, even absolution,
while the selfish Present scampers free.

45

Portrait of the Artist as a Youth Abroad

in Scotland, 1968

Wind lifts my hair, the sea's white hem
    that sweeps along the shore;
        it sleeks the banks
    of bonny dunes, the eel grass,
marram grass and thistle, spikes of fir.

A notebook in my hand, a book of verse
    in my slick coat, I'm ready for
        what takes me
    unawares, a faltering but fond
engagement with the tongue's unruly texture.

Hopkins, Yeats: the fathers on my knee,
    I mouth the rhythms that assume
        a correspondent
    world, wherein the tide-wrack strewn
on shingle spells survival, what's been saved.

Their language shatters in my head, sifts
    down, as surf through shingle
        glistens, and is gone.
    What's left? I wonder, dryly,
as the rough scarp rasps in salty wind.

Is this, then, life? I ask myself aloud.
    To stand in line, repeating
        what's been said
    and thought before, to rescue
nothing from the easy gold of water over sand.

Another morning in the pink-eyed dawn, I find
    myself alone, out walking

        on the sands, fists
    in my pockets, pages closed,
all memory at bay. It happens here.

Awash in syllables, in tides of sense,
    I bristle as the wet-backed
        words begin
    to roll past bladder wrack and kelp,
the whorling turrets of a thousand shells.

Portrait of the Artist as a Young Professor

in New Hampshire, 1975

It is always yellow on the sun-limned paths
   of mid-September as I walk
     to class: a seminar
   in Milton's broad excursion
through the ways we make all gardens fail us.

It is always shining in the uncut grass
   where Youth malingers in a fond
     absorption, self-
   deceived or self-dissembling, half
believing in its foolish gestures toward the sun.

It is always hopeful as I come before them,
   big book open, as I wait
     for thunder-blast,
   for heart-struck mind to reel,
for silence to cohere within their world.

It is always less than I had hoped for
   as I mouth the words, repeating
     the bright lines
   I cast, most days, like flies
upon a stream with nothing in its swirl.

It is always hard, how long the class is,
   how faces loom: bespeckled
     boys, the girls
   behind a curtain of damp hair,
all swearing it was Eve's fault that we fell.

It is always late when I walk home
   between the pines, lie down

        in sheets as stale
    as arguments against the Fall,
with memory's dead weight upon my chest.

It is always sad, that pool of dark,
    those soft leaves falling
        on the world's dry skin,
    the red-veined language broken
from a branch I shook against the sky.

Portrait of the Artist in Early Middle Age

in Bangkok, 1985

This is no postcard, honey, as the light
   drips over me, and no birds sing
     above my head,
   big bare brown knees, my own,
still baking as I sit beside the pool.

The idle rich! I'm one of them today,
   within the Oriental's glade,
     a grand hotel,
   the likes of which I never see
back home, where Rich is always Other,

and where light is dry: not this wet slurp
   of cross-hatched beams, a liquid
     netting like
   a steamy silk from some
old wet dream dreamt in youth, where sex—

like sweat in Bangkok—bled through everything:
   one's bedroom sheets, one's pants,
     one's hankies.
   This is called adulthood,
paunch and all, oppressed by shadowless and straight-up

noon, plateau of life, from which both sides,
   the Past and Future, represent
     decline, a falling
   off from this famed peak.
Is this, then, what I've always hoped for?
.

Do I understand exactly why I've come
   to Bangkok or become a father
      or have lost
   my hair? Do I deceive myself
like all the others, whom I once thought dull,

incapable of heights or depths of soul,
   the vulgar mob; *odi et arceo,*
      as Horace said,
   that prince of language
in whose dainty steps I've trod, do tread,

will tread forever until Death or, worse,
   Dementia absorb my impulse
      to put words
   to things, to make constructions,
verbal objects to contain my thoughts,

to pry the chrysalis of silence open,
   that most fertile crescent
      wherein, alas,
   all good things grow,
like poetry or sex or, even, money.

I am just too young or just too old
   to waste myself like this,
      to let my body
   simply boil away. If only
I could lose this abject cadence, maybe lose

this mask, maturity, which weighs upon
   my frame, this fleshly costume
     I assume each day
    as if it fit, God knows
I'd fly, yea, thither and beyond these words.

Portrait of the Artist as Paterfamilias

in Italy, 1986

How often in the dark I've seen that face,
  not mine, my father's
    as he skimmed the night
    from puffy cheeks at six A.M.,
his face a rosy oval in the mirror

as I watched him fondly, clutched his knees,
  and saw him as a man
    of God who ruled
    benignly over those he loved;
I feel my father in my skin today.

My elder son walks toward me in the dawn,
  a toddler in his shorts
    demanding juice;
    I draw myself toward the middling
height I've long since mastered and I take his hand.

The baby wakens as I pass his crib,
  and, blissfully, I smell
    the bloom of pride—
    a foolish father, who would steal
both boys to Timbuktu in twenty years

if anyone, our President or King,
  declared a war and wanted
    their sweet bodies
    in a line of fire. They bait me
over breakfast, scrambling for attention,

raiding my small hoard of Inner Peace.
  That rope of patience I have
      wound for years
    seems short today—no slack—
I slap the eldest child, the baby squeals.

Tears, idle tears. I kiss them both
  and wonder if my father
      likewise faked
    authority. Perhaps I misremember
how he seemed to rule with so few words?

I sit here in the bath an hour later,
    the baby in my arms,
      his brother dashing
    water on my head, and try to guess
if ever they'll recall my foolish ways,

how easily undone I was most days,
    unable to contain my rage
      sometimes, sometimes
    controlled, a veritable tower
of composure that they loved to storm.

Portrait of the Artist as an Old Man

in Vermont, 2038

In the dark glass, forward, the abysmal time
   to come, you read your visage
     in memorial mind,
    a broad-domed squire
leaning on a cane, a wide-brimmed hat

pulled rakishly across a sun-burned patch
   of flaking skin, a brow
     whose clench
    betrays impatience with a world
abandoned to its foolish self so many times.

At sunset, at great height, you watch the hawk
   scythe down the shadows
     of another day,
    admiring how it hangs there,
steady in the wind that whets its wings.

You think of Thomas Hardy, Yeats and Graves—
   the grand old men—of dear
     Red Warren,
    friend and mentor, whom you loved
to love, or Frost: Old Rocky Face himself.

I'm one of them, you say, and hope, lips smacking,
   drooling, one might say, still
     recomposing
    in your heart a life you've since
revised ten thousand times, no version

truer than the one before, or so it seems.
  Oh, how can you forget
    so many facts,
  the petty hatreds, fears, the fond
betrayals, posturings, reprisals—worse?

Maybe nothing matters but the final gloss,
  that beautifully wrought,
    penultimate
  revision made before the dark
blots every word, and heaven, like a blank page,

shines pristinely but, unlike before,
  needs no embossing, none of this
    black print
  you think adds something
to a paltry silence you cannot endure.

On midnight's mountain, in a cloak of stars,
  you look for answers to
    strong questions
  posed, a little falsely, re-
composed each day like shopping lists or prayers.

Will you ever know if any of those guises—
  hawk or mole, the fox,
    sweet ingenue,
  the rake or fool, the wise old man—
meant anything beyond their deft performance?

Will anyone replace the shattered hours,
    those pitiable shards which,
        reassembled
    in the bright Beyond, might
constitute, at last, a kind of heaven?

Portrait of the Artist Underground

in 2063

The roots become him, in their timeless thrall,
  the delicate and wormlike
    shoots of green
  that seem to bind him but which
set him free, loose through the ground.

He has no more need of calculation,
  love or money, even
    paltry things
  like bread or water; he has all
he wants of endlessly recurring lotus-silence,

which he takes for song, of dark and light,
  the lavish shadows, suns
    that drill the rock
  and liberate the vapor soul,
whatever in the last completes his shining.

He is past redemption, past regret
  for petty misdemeanors,
    crimes of passion,
  civilized commitments to
those guises which conceal the hungry heart.

His heart is left with only what it loved,
  and loved entirely,
    woman in
  one name, the beautiful
redoublings, words he gardened into silence,

which was his last shrine, his bo tree, blooming
  in the soil today, its

petal flowers
  flimsy and delicious on
his lips and eyelids, palms, the dirt, the wetness

that confirms this world, that speaks for everything
   now quick and running, while
      he lords it
   over, in the Lord-won air,
all men and women in the selfsame stare.

IV

Divine Parameters

Divine Parameters

The gull floats into the sun and flares,
a spray of sparks.
                    The wind says nothing.

Now you understand time's only end,
with distance as the way from here to there,
a leap across the dark from fire to fire.

Solstice, Entering Capricorn

In far-off states, the snow is falling
over silent fields that hide
the missiles, blue deer

running in the frozen woods behind the wind,
the winter apples black as figs,
choke cherries buried

in the plates of ice beyond recall.
In submarines, off shore, sub-zero weather,
warheads sleep

like prehistoric fish with one eye open.
Hammerheads move slowly through the depths;
the minnows darken.

Wolves tug firmly on their leash of sound
in Russian steppes
as bombers wait in icy hangars,

pilots shiver through the dreamless sleep
of those on call.
The black crows gather overhead in minds

of mice and rabbits. Spinning
in an ether all its own,
the earth knows nothing of its slow disease

as Capricorn, the goat-horn, digs
for spring, unable to contain its forward
tilt, its ignorant religion.

This Kampuchea

We sit in a *tuk-tuk* with binoculars,
sipping Fantas, as a hot white wind
blows over water half a mile wide—
a heat that most of us can just abide.
Pale tourists, young voyeurs: we find
humidity a subject. Kids with scars

across their cheeks and narrow backs beg
candies, cigarettes. We give them coins
that mean so little we can hardly not afford
to give them up. Such charity! I pour
my Fanta in a cup and give a swig
to a small boy whose mother joins

us from behind a shack, an improvised
bamboo construction housing refugees.
She hasn't said a word since she escaped,
the doctor tells us. Maybe she was raped
at knifepoint, maybe she had seen the trees
strung out with villagers Pol Pot despised

for simply being there. Then we all hear
they shot her husband in a ditch before her eyes;
her eyes seem blank now, darkly blank.
I notice that she never seems to blink
but watches like the bald-eyed moon, in fear,
as children utter their unlovely cries

for candy, cigarettes, for sips of Fanta
from my tinny cup. The bamboo clicks

in big-finned leaves across the river where
Cambodia has turned in its despair
to Kampuchea, where the golden bricks
of Angkor Wat sink like Atlantis

into jungle depths, the lost bright heart
of ancient quietude that's since been drowned
in spit and blood. I wonder why we came
to this sad border and if we're to blame
as much as anyone in that swart
jungle where the millions died as Death found

easy entrance on the world, engorged
itself, while faces turned another way.
Lon Nol, Pol Pot, the bloated Princes
whom the Rouge detested: none convinces
us that he's to blame. We'll never say
"this one" or "that" and feel relieved, purged

and guiltless, free to sail by 747
home to seasons in the hills of ease.
This Kampuchea has become a tomb
inside me, alien, but still a home
in some strange way—an altar where my knees
will fall at intervals, an odd chance given

to me as a gift, a place to bow
in obeisance to the darkest gods
who rule the heart whenever we ignore
our greatest charge: to watch and pray. The shore-

line glistens as a boy lets down a bamboo
rod, an old man settles by a tree and nods

off into dreams, a flame-bright bird
sails over water without any sense
of human borders. Children scurry to a jeep
beside us where the spoils are greater, as we keep
to schedule and drive away: untold expense
now memorized as what we saw and heard.

Things of This World

Reality inheres in particulars, of course,
but the problem is so many seem to buzz
around us, flash and fade, how can we know
which hold a decent quotient of the world,
enough to satisfy our wish to find
some intimations of the life to come?
That tree stump seeping by your foot, for instance,
could well be the perfect lopped-off symbol
of a life lived out; its seventy-three rings
so nicely mirror our three score plus ten:
the old allotment that we try to stretch
with better diets, exercise and will.
But there, against the mudbank, lies a muskrat,
dead as any deadhead tree and surely
in its way exemplary as well.
So why did it expire? What can it mean?
The questions that a four-year-old might ask
seem relevant near forty as I stand here
and assess my fate against these woods,
this river with its milky banks, this piece of sky.
I impose a thought upon each object
and expect a miracle of correlation:
worlds well met and mutually limning
Truth and Beauty, correspondent terms.
But weather more than objects may contain
the parallels we seek: the fine details
that represent a million different moods—
the way a raindrop hesitates in fog
could, for example, represent the way
most good ideas hover in a haze,
not quite released into the air until

a chill condenses them to fact—wet,
tangy and resolved. One could go on.
Snow is, observe, God's greatest gift
to poets of New England, endlessly imperfect
in its fallen state, its crystal forms,
a silence like the pause between right words,
amenable to every worldly surface, icing
on the cake of things. But weather, of itself,
is far too fragile to compete head on
with landscapes, vistas, Nature's present
to the active mind in search of objects
to contain its love, those hardy parallels
and fine, hard lines, those shapes amorphous
as a Rorschach blot, susceptible
to every little turn a thought could take.
One finds these sights most often in the woods,
that crackling plenitude of wholesome signs—
the black geese honking to the south again
in mid-September, taking with them song
but not its rippling echo in our voice.
We sing their going and adore the tune,
the poem of loss, articulately finding
what seems missing in the air itself,
as if our central purpose were to mourn
all separations: words and objects severed
by a moment's glance their way, the lone bird
rising and the bird we name—just not the same.
But why shed tears about a bird and not
a wheatfield ready to be mown, that sense of harvest
not as culmination but as something lost,
like high school graduations, where the parent mourns

the vacant bed, the empty places at supper,
as the band plays on? Each word we say
becomes an elegy to what is lost,
as this raw tree stump recollects the shade
we still remember from a Sunday picnic
when the world was green and parents played
and sorrow was the last thing left to learn.
Ah, words: we say them and we sigh . . .
Think how much sadness dictionaries hold,
a thousand pages of unending grief!
Perhaps the harvest scene as something lost
could be revised as victory, a prelude
to a cozy winter night beside the fire,
the lapdog lapping, children in their beds,
and moonlight in uplifted arms of trees.
The sparrows in the snow might well replace
the honking geese as something to admire:
tenacious little birds who just hang on,
like nettles in a wood or winter colds.
I like their blunt refusal to be budged,
the way they call up other stubborn things:
the high Norwegian pines that line this shore,
the stony outcrops that have never changed
in umpteen years, blue sky above the clouds,
the river which in every season moves
toward conclusion in some far-off sea.

Spring as an Example

The seasons shred around us, multiply
by simple subdivision into many parts;
we call this spring, for instance, in Vermont,
though the category lacks real definition.
The end of winter is a spring of sorts,
with rivulets that course beneath the ice
and crimson skies suggesting that tomorrow
could be warmer till you're hit with snow
(so different from the dry-flaked January stuff)
that clings like wet confetti to your coat
and melts to slush soon after breakfast.
The first good whiff of what we mean by spring
in normal conversation comes thereafter,
with its blowzy gusts from southern regions
with attendant birds, the gray-tipped woodlands
thinking green. But spring's a scurrilous
and rude backslider, miserable for those,
the pure at heart, who prefer the world redeemed
one time and once forever; spring retreats
into its early selves, its previous
and sodden incarnations, half convinced
it never could reform itself enough
to hold for long that pose identified
for ages by the name of spring. Like all
who lack whatever it may take to stand
behind their better selves, spring can't be trusted.
I've seen wild flowers parading for a week
in luminously gold, glad-handing weather,
only to be slain like Russian peasants
who defied the Tzar. The ghastly stories
multiply through March and into April,

when the mudtime comes in varied shades
of muddy red, mud-brown, mud-blue, and each
might claim a label of its own if English
had the wit to subdivide its famous quarters
and to house the seasons which must now go begging.
Mudtime surely would deserve at least
a foyer or a large back porch, if we
had properly conceived what mud has meant
to people in the fluid course of time;
it suggests sheer evil to the cunning linguist
who can trace its roots to Indo-European,
where the word for evil is the same as mud,
and the word for mud the same as feces,
as Freud has doubtless somewhere pointed out.
But this fatal linking of a human function
with the darker realms has hurt us badly;
we assume small guilts too easily
and leap from flesh to spirit as if one
were nasty and the other nice, especially
in mudtime, when we rue the day our souls
entered the body and became mere flesh,
susceptible to every passing whim
of that god, Weather, who commands our moods
and seems to make us pay for loveliness
with sorrows, tit for tat. Yet which of us
would dwell on mudtime when it's May and ferns
unfurl? When apple trees and hawthorn bloom
in yards and yellowhammers stitch the sky
with shrieks and goldfinch blaze like matchtips
on the hedge? Which of us would say, okay,
let's have one season, which is level: none

of this revolting up-and-down? We want
the multiples of spring and fall, the rise
of summer and the death of fall, but in between
we want the separately colored strands,
the warp of weather on the weft of time,
the endlessly revised and changing text
of each new season that requires a name
or temporary label. We have no real use
for categories broad beyond the flux
of hourly divisions or the buds that flare
in sudden sunlight and go dark by dusk,
or successive waves of migratory birds
that flap and fill the lucency of skies
with further shinings. So the seasons
shred, and every shred is evidence of life,
the life we live in multiples of seconds,
endlessly revising what's been given
as we lunge toward what may occur,
all irrespective of the final sum,
that one great name that everyone shall wear
when every season is subsumed in some
high summery and windless time above all time.

At the Ice Cream Parlor

Maybe it doesn't matter, but this chair—
black curlicues of iron, ice cream–parlor
perfect with its plastic seat and legs
right out of Paris in the Gilded Age—
reminds me of the one and only chair
that Plato dreamed of in his abstract heaven,
lofty and original and pure,
where every single noun is past declension,
where all men are Man, and Wolf is feral
to the *n*th degree, where Oak knows nothing
of November's claim upon its leaves,
its dainty little hands aquiver in
a blue, long-winded Breeze at noon forever,
while the Brook runs by with saucy stories
of the life upriver lively on its tongue,
as if bright gossip were the only end
of light and water, pebbles and white sand.
So all these things set out before me—
peppercorns and napkins, spoons, white bowls—
exist as versions of their final selves
(refracted in the dark receding mirrors,
a *mise-en-abîme* of checkered tablecloths
and sundry guests with lavish sundaes),
and each new spoon or peppercorn or bowl
or whatnot idles in its mere potential,
wondering if any bold recension
will effect the change to end all change.

Yet I sometimes wonder if we have the right
to postulate an ultimate revision
of each blessed thing, ignoring how

each object seems quite settled in its way,
not obviously hoping to progress
to some new state. One might as well propose
that everything delights in what it is,
its thingy presence, or at least accepts
what has been given and ignores our pompous,
motherly demand for something more.
Duns Scotus was, of course, appalled
that finer objects in the world's demesne
should have to be subjected to such pressure;
we ought to understand that sheer discreteness
is a good itself, the great sage thought,
conceiving of a neatly fretted world
where each leaf shimmers on each separate tree
without regard to anyone's conception
of a Tree or Leaf, each discontinuously
blazing forth like these black chairs, these bowls
and peppercorns and napkins, plastic spoons.
I probably would like a world like that,
where pebbles in the local gargling brook
aspired to nothing but their gargling selves,
where every flower was its own condition,
brittle and as bright as day could manage
but no more or less, and where each creature
was a thing apart, an entity composed
yet still composing, with successive states
discretely happy without longing toward
some final version in some perfect sky.

That notion of creation satisfies
our need to love what's here, to value time's

sweet local nimbus as a holy thing,
but only for a while. We begin too soon
to long for something we can barely scry,
to read for essences in what's been given
and resent the sense of time as present
and not past as well, the loss of future
as a light toward which all things grow.

The self that I admit each day in passing
(if I may divert this to myself)
is a paltry fellow, prone to narrowness
and self-regard, unwilling to add
charity most times to faith and hope,
and even faith has mostly to go begging
in a little heart that can't expand
without exertion and which rarely opens
to the world at large. The self I live with
is too mean to show, so lives disguised
in raiments of good fellowship and niceness,
decency and truth. He's proudly crafty
in the way he works, a fond dissembler
who has done more harm than anyone
would guess who didn't know, though I dismiss
him in my better moments and go off alone,
but only with that vision in my head
of his Big Brother up in Plato's sky,
a sort of guardian or souped-up angel
who regards me fondly from afar
and faintly through the milky glass of heaven
offers me a glimmer of fresh hope,
a finer version of the self I show,

a last recension I may only know
by lofting thither some appointed day.

Right now, I'm happy to believe that once
released from guilt and pressures to conform
or change my mind, free of all petty notions
of position, pride, or valor, I'll find myself
at peace beside all others in their final draft,
the absolute in hand that I have glimpsed
in offhand moments in unlikely places
(such as this dim parlor with its ice cream
chairs and tacky tables and recessive mirrors
that track a semblance of the man I am).
I'm happy to believe that every object
may well have the chance to change its name,
to clarify its essence and become
more like itself than nature will allow
in these rough drafts, these early versions
of that fabled state, the life to come.

Grandmother in Heaven

In a plume-field, white above the blue,
she's pulling up a hoard of rootcrops
planted in a former life and left to ripen:
soft gold carrots, beets, bright gourds.
There's coffee in the wind, tobacco smoke
and garlic, olive oil and lemon.
Fires burn coolly through the day,
the water boils at zero heat.
It's always almost time for Sunday dinner,
with the boys all home: dark Nello,
who became his cancer and refused to breathe;
her little Gino, who went down the mines
and whom they had to dig all week to find;
that willow, Tony, who became so thin
he blew away; then Julius and Leo,
who survived the others by their wits alone
but found no reason, after all was said,
for hanging on. They'll take their places
in the sun today at her high table,
as the antique beams light up the plates,
the faces that have lately come to shine.

At the Ruined Monastery in Amalfi

for Charles Wright

On a hill, approaching Easter,
well above the sea's bland repetitions
of the same old story
and the town's impenitent composure,
I survey old grounds.

The fire-winged gulls engulf the tower.
Lesser grackles, nuns and tourists,
scatter on the grass.

The brandy-colored light of afternoon
seeps through the stonework;
creeping flowers buzz and flutter
in the limestone cracks.

Wisteria-choked loggias drip with sun.

A honeycomb of cells absorbs the absence
it has learned to savor;
court and cloister close on silence,
the auroral prayers long since burned off
like morning fog.

The business of eternity goes on behind our backs.

In the chapel dark,
I'm trying to make out a worn inscription
on a wind-smudged altar,
but the Latin hieroglyphs have lost their edge.

Remember me, *Signore,*
who has not yet learned to read your hand,
its alphabet of buzz and drip and flutter.